First World War
and Army of Occupation
War Diary
France, Belgium and Germany

32 DIVISION
Divisional Troops
Loyal North Lancashire Regiment
12th Battalion Pioneers
1 March 1919 - 31 October 1919

WO95/2385/4

The Naval & Military Press Ltd
www.nmarchive.com
Published in association with The National Archives

Published by

The Naval & Military Press Ltd

Unit 10 Ridgewood Industrial Park,

Uckfield, East Sussex,

TN22 5QE England

Tel: +44 (0) 1825 749494

www.naval-military-press.com

www.nmarchive.com

This diary has been reprinted in facsimile from the original. Any imperfections are inevitably reproduced and the quality may fall short of modern type and cartographic standards.

© **Crown Copyright**
Images reproduced by permission of The National Archives, London, England, 2015.

Contents

Document type	Place/Title	Date From	Date To
Miscellaneous	WO95/2385 32 Division 12th Btn Loyal North Lancs March 1919 Oct 1919		
Heading	32 Div, Lancashire Division Coy. (Late 32nd Divn) 12 Loy Nth Lancs (P) Mar. Oct. 12th Bn Loyal Nth Lancs (Pioneers) 1919 Mar-Oct 1919 From 74 Div Troops France		
Miscellaneous	To/-Headquarters, 'A', Lancashire Division.	02/04/1919	02/04/1919
Heading	War Diary of 12th Bn Loyal North Lancs Regt (Pioneers) 1st March 1919 to 31st March 1919 Volume 34		
War Diary		01/03/1919	31/03/1919
Miscellaneous	To:- Headquarters, 'A', Lancashire Division.	01/05/1919	01/05/1919
Heading	War Diary of 12th Bn Loyal North Lancashire Regt (Pioneers) 1st April 1919 to 30th April 1919 (Volume 35)		
War Diary		01/04/1919	30/04/1919
Miscellaneous	To:- Lancashire Division. 'A'.		
Heading	War Diary of 12th. Battalion Loyal North Lancashire Regt. (Pioneers). 1st. May, 1919 to 31st. May, 1919 (Volume 36).		
War Diary		01/05/1919	31/05/1919
Miscellaneous	To:- Lancashire Division. A.	03/07/1919	03/07/1919
Heading	War Diary Of 12th. Bn. Loyal North Lancashire Regt. (Pioneers) 1st June, 1919 to 30th. June 1919. (Volume 37.)		
War Diary		01/06/1919	30/06/1919
Miscellaneous	To:- Lancashire Division A.	01/08/1919	01/08/1919
Heading	War Diary of 12th. Bn. Loyal North Lancashire Regt. (Pioneers). 1st. July, 1919 to 31st. July, 1919 (Volume 38)		
War Diary		01/07/1919	31/07/1919
Miscellaneous	To. Lancashire Division "A".	01/09/1919	01/09/1919
Heading	War Diary of 12th Bn Loyal North Lancs Regt (Pioneers) From 1st August 1919 to 31st August 1919. (Vol.39)		
War Diary	Dottendorf	01/08/1919	01/08/1919
War Diary	Nr Bonn	02/08/1919	30/08/1919
War Diary	Dottendorf	31/08/1919	31/08/1919
Miscellaneous	To. Lancashire Division "A"	29/09/1919	29/09/1919
Heading	War Diary Of 12th. Bn The Loyal North Lancashire. Regiment. 1st September To 30th September 1919. Volume. 40		
War Diary	Infantry Barracks, Argelander Strasse, Bonn.	01/09/1919	30/09/1919
Miscellaneous	To. Lancashire Division. "A"	01/11/1919	01/11/1919
War Diary	Infantry Barracks, Argelander Strasse, Bonn.	01/10/1919	17/10/1919
War Diary	Museum Barracks Coblenzer Strasse, Bonn.	18/10/1919	31/10/1919

WO 95/2365

32 DIVISION

12th Btn LOYAL NORTH LANCS

MARCH 1919 - OCT 1919

32 DIV. LANCASHIRE DIVISION Loy. Nth Lancs (P)
(LATE 32ND DIVN) Mar - Oct

12TH BN LOYAL NTH LANCS
(PIONEERS)
1914   MAR-OCT 1919

FROM 74 DIV TROOPS
FRANCE

No. A. 298.

To:- Headquarters, 'A',
    Lancashire Division.

I beg to forward herewith 'War Diary' for the month of March. 1919.

The copy is being sent direct to Home Records.

2/4/19.

O. Commanding,
12th. Loyal North Lancashire Regt. (Pioneers).

Army Form C. 2118.

WAR DIARY
or
INTELLIGENCE SUMMARY.
(Erase heading not required.)

Confidential

War Diary

of

12. Bn. Loyal North Lancs. Regt. (Pioneers)

1st March 1919 to 31st March 1919.

(Volume 34)

WAR DIARY
or
INTELLIGENCE SUMMARY.
(Erase heading not required.)

Army Form C. 2118.

Place	Date	Hour	Summary of Events and Information	Remarks and references to Appendices
	1919		Distribution	
	Mar. 1		Headquarters & 'A' Company billeted in POTTENDORF.	
			B & C Companies billeted in KESSINEGH	
			Morning - Company Training. Afternoon Organised	
	2		Recreational Training & Football	
			Coy C. & HQ. Church Parades in the morning	
	3.4.5		Each morning from 0900 to 1200 hours Section, Platoon &	
	6.7.8		Company Drill. Afternoons Recreational & Football	
			(Inter Platoon & Company)	
	4		3 ORs left for 14 days leave in the UK	
			All ORs of the Battalion bathed in the town Baths.	
			Bo-no-	
	5		2/Lt f. Y. Anacoon left the Battalion for 14 days ordinary	
			leave in UK	

WAR DIARY
or
INTELLIGENCE SUMMARY.
(Erase heading not required.)

Army Form C. 2118.

Instructions regarding War Diaries and Intelligence Summaries are contained in F. S. Regs., Part II. and the Staff Manual respectively. Title pages will be prepared in manuscript.

Place	Date	Hour	Summary of Events and Information	Remarks and references to Appendices
	1919			
	5		2/Lt. J. A. Thomas left the Unit to report to No. 3 Traffic Control Company	
	7		2/Lt. W.V. Grave left the Unit to attend the Fourth Course of Instruction at Trinity College, Oxford, commencing 4th March 1919	
	8		Lieuts. G.S. Harris, J.E. Cornell, 2nd Lieuts. J.B. Tone, C.J. Sollett all wished. J.W. Bainbridge, H. Stephenson M.M., S. Mellineer M.J. Crane M.C. G.W. Hellewell, & V.R. Harvey & 243 other ranks reported from the 1st Bn. Loyal North Lancashire Regt.	
	9		C of E & R.C. Services held in the morning	
	10, 11		Company training. Musketry etc. carried out each morning	
	12, 13	9.00 to 12.00 hours	Each afternoon Recreational Training & football	
	10		Lieuts. A. Dawson, R.P. Hargreaves & 2/Lts. J.H. Tacker and 50 O.R.s reported from the 2/4th Bn. Loyal North Lancs Regt.	
			10 O.R.s reported from the 1st Bn. Loyal North Lancs Regt.	
	12		Lts. C.A. Atkins & Col. Slack & 34 O.R.s reported from the 2/5 Bn. Loyal N. Lancs Regt. J.L. Pritchard & W. Strang. 2/Lt. J. Bonnington	
			Lieut. E.U. Ravilion	

WAR DIARY
INTELLIGENCE SUMMARY.
(Erase heading not required.)

Army Form C. 2118.

Place	Date	Hour	Summary of Events and Information	Remarks and references to Appendices
	1919			
	13.		H.V. Carver, H.F. Gibbs, J.E. Higgins, E.R. Schofield, W.E. Ulyatt, C.W. Donnellan, J.R. Scott & W.E. Knowles M.M. & 166 ORs reported from the 2nd Bn Loyal North Lancs Regt. Half the Battalion visited the Town Baths. Coy. for # bathing in the afternoon. The Battalion was inspected by the G.O.C. 32nd Division (Major General Y.S. Lambert C.B. C.M.G.)	
		14.	14 ORs reported from the 1st Bn Loyal North Lancs Regt. 3 ORs reported from the 2nd Bn Loyal North Lancs Regt. 14 ORs left for 14 days leave in UK Lt S.H. Bailey reported back from duty from the III Corps Agricultural School.	
		15.	Section & Platoon Drill in the morning Recreational training in the afternoon. Lt. J.R. Young & 2/Lt W. Lochwaite reported from the 2/5 L. Bn Loyal North Lancs Regt	

WAR DIARY
or
INTELLIGENCE SUMMARY.
(Erase heading not required.)

Army Form C. 2118.

Instructions regarding War Diaries and Intelligence Summaries are contained in F.S. Regs., Part II. and the Staff Manual respectively. Title pages will be prepared in manuscript.

Place	Date	Hour	Summary of Events and Information	Remarks and references to Appendices
	1919			
	16		Lieut J.E.S. Boage & M.R. Muddleton & 2/Lt C.W. Duckley left the Unit to report to the 15th Bn. Loyal North Lancs Regt. Lieut J.L. Pritchard, 2/Lieuts J.E. Higgins, F. Bonnington & S. Westwood, C.R. Cologues M.C. left the Unit to report to the 2/5th Bn Loyal North Lancs Regt. Lieut J.E. Moore & 2/Lieuts L.E. Sowitt left the unit to report to the 1/5th Bn Loyal North Lancs Regt. Two ORs left the unit for 14 days leave in UK	
	16		Col C.E & R.C. Servais held in the morning. Companies carried out Platoon & Company Drill each morning from 0900 to 1200 hrs. Each afternoon organised Recreational Training & Football Matches. During the wk. all ORs of the Battalion bathed at the Lower Baths, Bonn.	
	17		1 OR left the Unit for transfer to Home Establishment. 1 OR left the unit for 14 days leave in UK	

Army Form C. 2118.

WAR DIARY
or
INTELLIGENCE SUMMARY.
(Erase heading not required.)

Instructions regarding War Diaries and Intelligence Summaries are contained in F. S. Regs., Part II. and the Staff Manual respectively. Title pages will be prepared in manuscript.

Place	Date	Hour	Summary of Events and Information	Remarks and references to Appendices
	1919			
	24.25.26 27.28.29		Two ORs reported for duty from the 1st Bn Loyal North Lancs Regt. Each morning from 0900 to 1200 hours, company carried out Sectional, Company, & Physical Training. In the afternoons, Recreational Training & Football Matches.	
		24	Capt E.E. Gough. R.A.M.C. reported for duty as Medical Officer in relief of Capt J. M. McLoughlin, M.O.R.C, U.S.A. who leaves for demobilization	
COBLENZ	26		A party of 25 officers & 200 ORs made a trip up the Rhine to Lieuts J Dawson M.C. & J.S. Barnes. 2/Lieuts R. Pride. W.R Bennett. R.S.M Hulme M.C., R.Q.M.S Latham and L/C. Minogue and 163 other ranks reported for duty from the 1/4th Bn. Loyal North Lancs Regt.	

Army Form C. 2118.

WAR DIARY
or
INTELLIGENCE SUMMARY.
(Erase heading not required.)

Instructions regarding War Diaries and Intelligence Summaries are contained in F. S. Regs., Part II. and the Staff Manual respectively. Title pages will be prepared in manuscript.

Place	Date	Hour	Summary of Events and Information	Remarks and references to Appendices
	1919			
	12		Lieut C.G. Nightingale & 4 ORs reported for duty from the 2nd Bn Loyal North Lancs Regt	
			Lieut G.W. Slack & 2/Lt C.R. Laker admitted to Hospital (V.D.)	
	13		Capt W. Manning M.M., Capt W.R. Watkins, Lieut P.G. Johnson & 2/Lt J. Hogg reported from the 15th Bn Loyal North Lancs Regt	
			Lieut J.R. Waugh & two ORs reported from the 1st Bn Loyal North Lancs Regt	
			Two ORs reported from the 2nd Bn Loyal North Lancs Regt	
			Three ORs left the unit to report back to their own Battalion (1st Bn Loyal North Lancs Regt) having been wrongly despatched	
			2/Lt S. Mulhearn admitted to Hospital sick	
	19		A party of 20 officers and 100 ORs made a trip up the Rhine to COBLENZ who occupied the whole day	
	20		A complete Educational Scheme for the Battalion was put into operation to day. Each Company will, in future, devote two mornings per week to Educational training every man	

(A7093). Wt. W12859/M1703. 75,3,0,0. 1/17. D.D. & L.,Ltd. Forms/C.2118/24.

WAR DIARY
or
INTELLIGENCE SUMMARY.

Army Form C. 2118.

Place	Date	Hour	Summary of Events and Information	Remarks and references to Appendices
	1919		excepting those specially employed, will attend.	
			Capt S.G. Flood reported for duty from the 16th Bn Loyal North Lancs Regt.	
			Lieut A Sumner, 2/Lt L & Stirling, AA Peterkin, WR Lyne, HV Coole reported for duty from the 1/5th Bn Loyal North Lancs Regt.	
			2/Lt LWope reported for duty from the 2/5th Bn Loyal North Lancs Regt.	
	21		Lieut EH Smith and 4 ORs reported from the 1st Bn Loyal North Lancs Regt.	
			Two ORs left the unit for 14 days leave in UK.	
	22		Capt HA Richardson, Lieut GR Walkden, & 2/Lt RL Crowther reported for duty from the 1/5th Bn Loyal North Lancs Regt.	
			Lieut J Wilkinson MM reported for duty from the 2/5th Bn Loyal North Lancs Regt.	
	23		6 Offrs & RC Service held in the morning.	
			2/Lt LG Anderson reported back from leave in UK	

Army Form C. 2118.

WAR DIARY
or
INTELLIGENCE SUMMARY.
(Erase heading not required.)

Instructions regarding War Diaries and Intelligence Summaries are contained in F. S. Regs., Part II. and the Staff Manual respectively. Title pages will be prepared in manuscript.

Place	Date	Hour	Summary of Events and Information	Remarks and references to Appendices
	25 1919		Lieut E Williamson reported for duty from the 2/5th Bn Loyal North Lancs Regt	
	26		2/Lt H.C. Crowther left for 14 days leave in UK	
			Lieut E.J. Hart left the Battalion to report to CRE 59th Division for attachment on probation.	
			Two ORs left for 14 days leave in UK	
	27		2/Lt S Hacking & 2 ORs reported for duty from 2nd Bn Loyal North Lancs Regt	
			The G.O.C. Lancashire Division (Major General Sir N.S. Jacdine K.C.B.) inspected the Battalion Transport, Billets, & Places of Instruction	
	28		The Commanding Officer (Lieut Col. W Langhorn) left for demobilization. Major J. Watkins, M.C. assumes Command of the Battalion.	

WAR DIARY
or
INTELLIGENCE SUMMARY.
(Erase heading not required.)

Army Form C. 2118.

Place	Date 1919	Hour	Summary of Events and Information	Remarks and references to Appendices
	29		2/Lt A Tyne left the Battalion to report to the D.G. I Bologne Station for duty as Train Conducting Officer	
			Lieut J.M. Heap & 6 ORs reported for duty from the 1st Bn Loyal North Lancs Regt	
			2/Lt J.J. Pendlebury reported for duty from the 15th Bn. Loyal North Lancs Regt	
			2/Lt S. Mullinese reported for duty from Hospital	
	30		C of E & R.C. Services held in the morning	
			Lieut H.J. Charles left the Battalion to report to Headquarters 14th Infantry Brigade for duty as Light Trench Mortar Instructor	
			Physical & Company Training & Musketry by Companies	
	31		From 0900 to 1200 hours. Afternoon Recreational Training	
			Lieut C.G. Nightingale DCM left the Battalion to report	

WAR DIARY
INTELLIGENCE SUMMARY.

Place	Date	Hour	Summary of Events and Information	Remarks and references to Appendices
	1919		To the Military Governor, Cologne, for duty as Assistant Town Major.	
			16 ORs reported from the 1/4th Bn Royal North Lancs Regt	
			20 ORs reported from the 2/5th Bn Loyal North Lancs Regt	

Army Form C. 2118.

Casualties - 1st to 31st March

Officers admitted to Hospital - sick   3
ORs   "   "   "   18
Officers returned to duty from Hospital 1
ORs   "   "   "   8

Strength - 31st March 1919.

68 Officers.
1265 Other Ranks.

> 12 Bn. LOYAL NORTH LANCS. REGT.
> **PIONEERS**
> 1 MAY 1919
> No. /

To:- Headquarters, 'A',
   Lancashire Division.

   I beg to forward herewith ~~copy of~~ 'War Diary' for the month of April, 1919.

R.T.Pelly Lieut. Colonel.
Commanding, 12th. Bn. Loyal North Lancashire Regt. (Pnrs).

Original.

Army Form C. 2118.

WAR DIARY
or
INTELLIGENCE SUMMARY.
(Erase heading not required.)

Confidential.

War Diary

of

12th Bn: Loyal North Lancashire Regt. (Pioneers)

1st April 1919 to 30th April 1919.

(Volume 35)

Army Form C. 2118.

WAR DIARY
or
INTELLIGENCE SUMMARY.
(Erase heading not required.)

Instructions regarding War Diaries and Intelligence Summaries are contained in F. S. Regs., Part II. and the Staff Manual respectively. Title pages will be prepared in manuscript.

Place	Date 1919	Hour	Summary of Events and Information	Remarks and references to Appendices
	Jan 1st		Distribution. Headquarters & B Company billeted in DOTTENDORF. A C & D Companies billeted in KESSINECH.	
	" 1st		Battalion practised taking up positions on the BONN BRIDGE. Reinforcements. 2 O.R's from the 1/4th L.N.Lancs Regt. 4 O.R's from the 1st L.N.Lancs Regt.	
	- 2nd		Company Training.	
	- 3rd		Company Training in the morning. Education in the afternoon. Reinforcements. Lt. W.H.Jones; 2/Lt. H.Murta & R.W.Robinson from the 2nd Bn. L.N.Lancs Regt. 3 O.R's from the 1/4th Bn. L.N.Lancs Regt.	
	- 4th		Company Training. 2/Lt. J.W. Bainbridge admitted to Hospital.	
	- 5th		Company Training in the morning. Two Platoons of "B" Coy. moved to RAMERSDORF for work under the 14th Brigade in the construction of Rifle Range &c. Reinforcements. 7 O.R's from the 2nd Bn. L.N.Lancs Regt.	

Army Form C. 2118.

WAR DIARY
or
INTELLIGENCE SUMMARY.
(Erase heading not required.)

Instructions regarding War Diaries and Intelligence Summaries are contained in F. S. Regs., Part II. and the Staff Manual respectively. Title pages will be prepared in manuscript.

Place	Date 1919	Hour	Summary of Events and Information	Remarks and references to Appendices
	April 6th		Lieut. S.H. Bailey was admitted to Hospital	
	" 7th		Usual Church Parade Services. 2/Lt. W. Towle reported from the 3rd Corps Concentration Camp from duty. Lieut. E. Williamson admitted to Hospital	
	" 8th		Company Training. 2/Lt. W. Towle & H.S. Scott being Regular Officers left for the UK to report to their respective Regimental Depots. Reinforcements. Lt. J. Stanley & 3. O/Rs. from the 1/4th Bn. L.N. Lancs. Regt. 2/Lt. O.H. Hall from the 1st Bn. L.N. Lancs Regt. Company Training Education. Reinforcements 13 O/Rs from the 2/5th Bn. L.N. Lancs. Regt. Lieut. S.H. Bailey returned Hospital	

Army Form C. 2118.

WAR DIARY
or
INTELLIGENCE SUMMARY.
(Erase heading not required.)

Instructions regarding War Diaries and Intelligence Summaries are contained in F. S. Regs., Part II. and the Staff Manual respectively. Title pages will be prepared in manuscript.

Place	Date 1919	Hour	Summary of Events and Information	Remarks and references to Appendices
	Apl. 9		Company training Education. Lieut. Col. J. McCarthy O'Leary took over command of the Battalion. 7/Lt. W. J. Gleave returned from course at Oxford.	
	10		Company training in the morning. Bathing in the afternoon.	
	11		Company training in the morning. Education bathing in the afternoon.	
	12		The Battalion paraded for Inspection by the C.O. 7/Lt. T. R. Smith returned from leave in U.K.	
	13		Usual Church Service	
	14		Company training in the morning. Educational training in the afternoon. Lieut. Col. R. J. Kelly C.M.G., D.S.O. assumed Command of the Battalion. Reinforcements: 46. O.R's from the 94th Bn. L.N. Lancs. Regt.	

Army Form C. 2118.

WAR DIARY
or
INTELLIGENCE SUMMARY.
(Erase heading not required.)

Instructions regarding War Diaries and Intelligence Summaries are contained in F. S. Regs., Part II. and the Staff Manual respectively. Title pages will be prepared in manuscript.

Place	Date	Hour	Summary of Events and Information	Remarks and references to Appendices
	1919 April 15th		Inspection of the Battalion by G.O.C. Lancashire Division.	
	16th		Company training in the morning. Reorganization of the Battalion in the afternoon.	
	17th		Companies interior economy all day.	
	18th		Lieut. J. Stanley admitted to Hospital. Sick was observed as a Holiday. Lieut. parades in the morning. Lieut. S. Williamson returned from Hospital.	
	19th		Company training in the morning.	
	20th		Usual Parade Services. 1st prisoners returned from leave.	
	21st		Company training in the morning. Educational training in the afternoon.	
	22nd		Company training in the morning. Educational training in the afternoon.	

Army Form C. 2118.

WAR DIARY
or
INTELLIGENCE SUMMARY.
(Erase heading not required.)

Instructions regarding War Diaries and Intelligence Summaries are contained in F.S. Regs., Part II. and the Staff Manual respectively. Title pages will be prepared in manuscript.

Place	Date 1919	Hour	Summary of Events and Information	Remarks and references to Appendices
	April 23		Company training in the morning. Educational training in the afternoon	
	24		Company training in the morning. Educational training in the afternoon. Lieut (A/Capt) B. Moore left the Battalion for demobilisation	
	25		Company training in the morning. Educational training in the afternoon	
	26		Company training in the morning. Capt. J. Watters M.C. left the Battalion for demobilisation. 2/Lt. J.R. Case Reinforcement from the 15th Bn. L.N. Lancs. Regt. reported for duty	
	27		Usual Church Parades.	
	28		Battalion inspected by the G.O.C. Lancs. Division as a rehearsal parade for the inspection by the C in C at the beginning of next week	

WAR DIARY
or
INTELLIGENCE SUMMARY.

(Erase heading not required.)

Army Form C. 2118.

Place	Date 1919	Hour	Summary of Events and Information	Remarks and references to Appendices
	April	30	Company training in the morning. Educational training in the afternoon. "A" Company left the Battalion for duty under the C.R.E. Army Troops. Their work is making Training Area at ELSENBORN. Company training in the morning. Educational training in the afternoon. Lieut. J. Stukeley reported back from Hospital. Lieut. S.H. Roades returned from leave in U.K.	

N.T. Kelly, Lt. Col.
Commdg. 12TH BN. LOYAL N. LANCS. REGT. (PIONEERS)

Army Form C. 2118.

WAR DIARY
or
INTELLIGENCE SUMMARY.
(Erase heading not required.)

Instructions regarding War Diaries and Intelligence Summaries are contained in F. S. Regs., Part II. and the Staff Manual respectively. Title pages will be prepared in manuscript.

Place	Date	Hour	Summary of Events and Information	Remarks and references to Appendices
			Casualties - 1st to 30th April 1919	
			Officers admitted to Hospital - sick - 3	
			O.R's " " " " - 47	
			Officers returned to duty from Hospital - 2	
			O.R.S " " " " - 26	
			Strength - 30th April 1919	
			76 Officers.	
			1339 Other Ranks.	

> 12 Bn. LOYAL NORTH LANCS. REGT.
> **PIONEERS**
> 1 JUN. 1919
> No. /   /

To:- Lancashire Division. 'A'.

      Herewith Original 'War Diary' for the Month of May, 1919, please.

R. T. Pelly   Lieut. Colonel.
                      Commanding.
12th. Bn. Loyal North Lancashire Regt. (Pioneers).

Army Form C. 2118.

WAR DIARY
or
INTELLIGENCE SUMMARY.

(Erase heading not required.)

ORIGINAL.

Instructions regarding War Diaries and Intelligence Summaries are contained in F. S. Regs., Part II. and the Staff Manual respectively. Title pages will be prepared in manuscript.

CONFIDENTIAL

WAR DIARY

OF

12th. Battalion, Loyal North Lancashire Regt. (Pioneers).

1st. May, 1919 to 31st. May, 1919.

(VOLUME 36).

Army Form C. 2118.

WAR DIARY
or
INTELLIGENCE SUMMARY.
(Erase heading not required.)

Instructions regarding War Diaries and Intelligence Summaries are contained in F. S. Regs., Part II. and the Staff Manual respectively. Title pages will be prepared in manuscript.

Place	Date 1919.	Hour	Summary of Events and Information	Remarks and references to Appendices
	May.			
	1.		DISTRIBUTION. Headquarters Company and Transport Section at DOTTENDORF. Half of 'B' Company, and half of 'C' Company at KESSENICH. 'A' Company at ELSENBORN. Oneplatoon of 'C' Company at MENDEN. One Platoon of 'C' Company at MEINDORF. Two Platoons of 'B' Company at RAMERSDORF.	
	2.		Training during the day.	
	3.		Company Training in the morning. Bathing in the afternoon.	
	4.		Kit Inspection in the morning. Cricket Match in the afternoon. 2/Lieut. W.W. Long, and one other rank reported from the 1/4th. Bn. L.N.Lancs. Rgt.	
	5/8.		Usual Church Services.	
	9.		Pioneering in the mornings. Education in the afternoons.	
	10.		Company Training in the morning. Bathing in the afternoon.	
	11.		Kit Inspection in the morning. Cricket Match in the afternoon.	
	12.		Church Services.	
	13/15.		Commander-in-Chief, British Army of the Rhine, inspected Lancashire Division in the EXERZIERPLATZ at 1000 hours. The Parade was under the Command of Brigadier General Frith, C.M.G., D.S.O., Commanding 2nd. Lancashire Brigade. 2nd. Bn. Loyal North Lancs. Regt. lent this unit their Band for the March-Past. Pioneering in the mornings. Education in the afternoons.	
	16.		Company Training in the morning. Bathing in the afternoon.	

Army Form C. 2118.

WAR DIARY
or
INTELLIGENCE SUMMARY.
(Erase heading not required.)

Instructions regarding War Diaries and Intelligence Summaries are contained in F. S. Regs., Part II. and the Staff Manual respectively. Title pages will be prepared in manuscript.

Place	Date 1919	Hour	Summary of Events and Information	Remarks and references to Appendices
	May			
	17.		R.S.M. Bretton. H.W., reported as reinforcement from the 11th. Manchester Regt. Three other ranks reinforcements from the Base. Kit Inspection in the morning. Cricket Match in the afternoon.	
	18.		Usual Church Services.	
	19/21.		Pioneering in the mornings. Education in the afternoons. The Education on the afternoon of the 21st. took the form of a Lecture by Lieut. Col. Tysham on "COUNTERACTING BOLSHEVISTIC TENDENCIES." This Lecture took place in the BEETHOVEN HALLE, BONN.	
	22/23.		Two O.R's Reinforcements reported from 1st. Bn. L.N.Lancs. Regt. on the 19th.inst. Working on the Dottendorf Range in the mornings. Bathing in the afternoons.	
	24.		Kit Inspection in the morning. Cricket Match in the afternoon.	
	25.		Usual Church Services.	
	26/28.		Working on the Dottendorf Range in the mornings. Education in the afternoons.	
	29.		Company Training in the morning. Bathing in the afternoon. Lessons in Country Dancing given by Y.M.C.A. ladies in the evening.	
	30.		Pioneering in the morning. Bathing in the afternoon. 2 Officers Reinforcements.- Capt. A. Bencini, 52nd. Kings Liverpool Regt. and Lieut. W.R. Godden from the 52nd. Manchester Regt.	
	31.		200 men of the Battalion went on the Rhine Steamer to COBLENZ for the day. The remainder of the Battalion had a Kit Inspection.	

Army Form C. 2118.

WAR DIARY
or
INTELLIGENCE SUMMARY.

(Erase heading not required.)

Instructions regarding War Diaries and Intelligence Summaries are contained in F. S. Regs., Part II. and the Staff Manual respectively. Title pages will be prepared in manuscript.

Place	Date 1919	Hour	Summary of Events and Information	Remarks and references to Appendices
	May.			
			CASUALTIES - 1st. May to 31st. May. 1919.	
			Officers admitted to Hospital - sick............nil. Other Ranks. do. do. ....27.	
			Officers returned to duty from Hospital.............3. Other Ranks. do. do. do. ....17.	
			STRENGTH.	
			74........Officers. 1325.......Other Ranks.	
			N.T.Pelly...Lieut.Colonel. Commanding.	
			12th. Bn. Loyal North Lancashire Regt. (Pioneers).	

```
12 BN. LOYAL NORTH LANCS. REGT.
PIONEERS
3 JUL. 1919
No. /............../..............
```

To:- Lancashire Division. A.

      Herewith original copy of 'War Diary' for the month of June, 1919.

                        R.T. Pelly   Lieut. Colonel.
                                  Commanding,
3/7/19.   12th. Bn. Loyal North Lancashire Regt. (Pioneers).

Army Form C. 2118.

WAR DIARY
or
INTELLIGENCE SUMMARY.
(Erase heading not required.)

CONFIDENTIAL

WAR DIARY

OF

12th. Bn. Loyal North Lancashire Regt. (Pioneers).

1st. June, 1919 to 30th. June, 1919.

(VOLUME 37.)

Army Form C. 2118.

WAR DIARY
or
INTELLIGENCE SUMMARY.
(Erase heading not required.)

Instructions regarding War Diaries and Intelligence Summaries are contained in F. S. Regs., Part II. and the Staff Manual respectively. Title pages will be prepared in manuscript.

Place	Date 1919.	Hour	Summary of Events and Information	Remarks and references to Appendices
	June.			
	1.		DISTRIBUTION.	
			Headquarters Company and Transport Section at DOTTENDORF. Half of B. Company and half of C. Company at KESSENICH. 'A' Company at ELSENBORN. One Platoon of C. Company at MENDEN. One Platoon of C. Company at MEINDORF. Two Platoons of B. Company at RAMERSDORF.	
	2.		Usual Church Services in the morning.	
			Pioneering in the morning. Lecture in the afternoon by THE REV HEASLETT, B.A.	
	3 & 4.		Company Parades.	
	5 & 6.		Battalion Parades.	
	7.		Interior Economy.	
	8.		Usual Church Services.	
	9.		Major (T/Lieut.Col.) W.H. Murphy, D.S.O., T.D., 17th. London Regt., reported for duty as 2nd. in Command vice Major (T/Lieut.Col.) J. MacCarthy O'Leary, South Lancs. Regt.,	
	9, 10 & 11)		Company Training.	
	12 & 13.		Battalion Parades.	
	14.		Interior Economy.	
	15.		Usual Church Services.	
	16.		A. Company on detachment at ELSENBORN returned to the Battalion.	

Army Form C. 2118.

WAR DIARY
or
INTELLIGENCE SUMMARY.
(Erase heading not required.)

Instructions regarding War Diaries and Intelligence Summaries are contained in F. S. Regs., Part II. and the Staff Manual respectively. Title pages will be prepared in manuscript.

Place	Date	Hour	Summary of Events and Information	Remarks and references to Appendices
	1919. June.			
	17.		Company Training. Winter Blanket issue withdrawn.	
	18.		Battalion went on Rhine River Pleasure Trip to COBLENZ.	
	19.		Battalion moved to the MONASTERY - SIEGBURG. Surplus Officers and other ranks were left behind at the Divisional Reception Camp.	
	20 & 21.		Battalion Parades.	
	22.		Usual Church Services in the morning. Concert in the evening.	
	23.		Battalion Parade.	
	24.		Company Parades.	
	25.		Battalion Parade.	
	26.		Company Parades.	
	27 & 28.		Battalion Parades.	
	29.		Usual Church Services in the morning. Concert in the evening.	
	30.		Battalion Parade.	

Army Form C. 2118.

WAR DIARY
or
INTELLIGENCE SUMMARY.
(Erase heading not required.)

Instructions regarding War Diaries and Intelligence Summaries are contained in F. S. Regs., Part II. and the Staff Manual respectively. Title pages will be prepared in manuscript.

Place	Date 1919.	Hour	Summary of Events and Information	Remarks and references to Appendices
	June.			
			CASUALTIES – 1st. June to 30th. June 1919.	
			Officers admitted to Hospital – sick...........1.	
			" " " " " ....61.	
			O.Rs.	
			Officers returned to Duty from Hospital..........nil.	
			O.Rs. " " " " ....33.	
			S T R E N G T H.	
			75............Officers.	
			1362...........Other Ranks.	
			A.T. Pell......Lieut. Colonel. Commanding.	
			12th. Bn. Loyal North Lancashire Regiment. (Pioneers).	

> 12 Bn. LOYAL NORTH LANCS. REGT.
> PIONEERS
> 1 AUG. 1919

C O N F I D E N T I A L.

To:- Lancashire Division A.

   Herewith original copy of 'War Diary' for the month of July, 1919.

              Lieut. Colonel.
               commanding,
     12th. Bn. Loyal North Lancashire Regt. (Pioneers).

Army Form C. 2118.

WAR DIARY
or
INTELLIGENCE SUMMARY.
(Erase heading not required.)

CONFIDENTIAL

WAR DIARY

OF

12th. Bn. Loyal North Lancashire Regt. (Pioneers).

1st. July, 1919 to 31st. July, 1919.

(VOLUME 38)

Army Form C. 2118.

WAR DIARY
or
INTELLIGENCE SUMMARY.
(Erase heading not required.)

Instructions regarding War Diaries and Intelligence Summaries are contained in F.S. Regs., Part II. and the Staff Manual respectively. Title pages will be prepared in manuscript.

Place	Date 1919. July.	Hour	Summary of Events and Information	Remarks and references to Appendices
KESSINICH.			DISTRIBUTION. Headquarters Company and Transport Section at DOTTENDORF. Companies at	
	1.		The Battalion returned to Dottendorf from Siegburg.	
	2.		The Battalion was given a day off in order to clean up.	
	3.		Battalion Parade to practice Ceremonial for the Presentation of the King's Colours.	
	4.		Battalion Parade to practice Ceremonial for the Presentation of the King's Colours.	
	5.		The Battalion formed up in mass in Hofgarten, Bonn, at 1000 hours to receive the Presentation, and Consecration of the King's Colours by Lieut General T.L. Morland, K.C.B., K.C.M.G., D.S.O., Commanding X Corps. This parade was a great success, and the Battalion was complimented both by the Corps and Divisional Commander for steadiness on parade.	
	6.		Usual Church Services.	
	7.		The Battalion held Sports in commemoration of the Presentation of the Colours.	
	8.		One Company completing the Dottendorf Range. Other two Companies - drill and Education. 14 surplus officers sent to U.K.	
	9.		Battalion commenced firing General Musketry Course on Dottendorf Range. Four surplus officers sent to U.K.	
	10.		Usual Company Training. One Surplus officer sent to U.K.	
	11.		Battalion Parade.	
	12.		The Battalion was given a holiday in order to attend the Cologne Race Meeting.	

Army Form C. 2118.

WAR DIARY
or
INTELLIGENCE SUMMARY.

(Erase heading not required.)

Instructions regarding War Diaries and Intelligence Summaries are contained in F. S. Regs., Part II. and the Staff Manual respectively. Title pages will be prepared in manuscript.

Place	Date 1919.	Hour	Summary of Events and Information	Remarks and references to Appendices
	July 13.		Usual Church Services.	
	14.		Battalion continued firing the G.M.C.	
	15.		One surplus officer sent to U.K.	
	16.		Continuance of G.M.C.	
	17.		Usual Company Training and Education.	
	18.		Battalion Sports.	
	19.		Battalion was given a holiday in commemoration of the Signing of Peace.	
	20.		Usual Church Services.	
	21st.		The Battalion was photographed by the Official Panoramic Photographer. One surplus officer sent to U.K.	
	22.		Usual Company training.	
	23.		Continuance of firing G.M.C.	
	24.		Usual Company Training.	
	25.		Usual Company Training.	
	26.		Usual Company Training.	
	27.		Usual Church Services.	
	28.		Lieut. Colonel R.T. Pally, C.B., C.M.G., D.S.O., ordered home to report to 1st. Battalion. L.N.Lancs. Major W.H. Murphy, D.S.O., T.D., assumed Command of the Battalion.	

Army Form C. 2118.

WAR DIARY
or
INTELLIGENCE SUMMARY.
(Erase heading not required.)

Instructions regarding War Diaries and Intelligence Summaries are contained in F.S. Regs. Part II. and the Staff Manual respectively. Title pages will be prepared in manuscript.

12th. Battalion, Loyal North Lancashire Regiment. (Pioneers).

Lieut. Colonel.
Commanding,

CASUALTIES - 1st. July, 1919 to 31st. July, 1919.

Officers admitted to Hospital - sick................ 1
Other Ranks " " " " .... 66.
Officers returned to Duty from Hospital............nil.
Other Ranks " " " " " ....78.

S T R E N G T H.

53.............Officers.
1338...........Other Ranks.

Place	Date	Hour	Summary of Events and Information	Remarks and references to Appendices
	1919 July 29.		Usual Company Training.	
	30.		Continuance of G.M.C.	
	31.		Usual Company Training.	

>   12 Bn. LOYAL NORTH LANCS. REGT.
>   **PIONEERS**
>   1 SEP. 19
>   No. 1

To:- Lancashire Division "A".

    Herewith original copy of War Diary for the month of August, please.

                                      Lieut. Colonel,
                                       Commanding,
        12th Bn. Loyal North Lancashire Regt. (Pioneers).

Original

Army Form C. 2118.

WAR DIARY
or
~~INTELLIGENCE SUMMARY.~~
(Erase heading not required.)

Confidential

War Diary

of

1st Bn. Royal North Lancs. Regt (Pioneers)

from 1st August 1919 to 31st August 1919.

(Vol 39)

Army Form C. 2118.

Original

WAR DIARY
or
INTELLIGENCE SUMMARY.
(Erase heading not required)

Place	Date 1919	Hour	Summary of Events and Information	Remarks and references to Appendices
DOTTENDORF	Aug. 1st		Distribution H.Q. & Transport at Dottendorf. Companies at KESSENICH.	
N. BONN	2nd		Usual Company training	
	3rd		Interior Economy	
	4th		Usual Church Service.	
	5th		Observed as a Holiday	
	6th		Usual Company training. Inter Company Boxing match. 'C' Company won.	
	7th		One company firing G.M.C. on range; remainder Usual Company training	
	8th		Usual Company training	
	9th		Batth Parade	
	10th		Lecture on "NIGERIA" by Mr Allan Upward.	
	11th		Usual Church Service.	
	12th		One Company firing G.M.C on range, remainder Usual Company training	
	13th		Usual Company training	
	14th		One Company firing G.M.C on range, remainder "	
	15th		Usual Company training	
	16th		Companies at disposal of Coy Commanders. Capt. H. OLLY joined as Quartermaster.	
	17th		Interior Economy	
	18th		Usual Church Service	
	19th		One Company firing G.M.E on range remainder Usual Company training	
	20th		Usual Company training	
			One Company firing in range (G.M.E) remainder Usual Coy training	

Original

Army Form C. 2118.

WAR DIARY
or
INTELLIGENCE SUMMARY.
(Erase heading not required.)

Instructions regarding War Diaries and Intelligence Summaries are contained in F. S. Regs., Part II. and the Staff Manual respectively. Title pages will be prepared in manuscript.

Place	Date	Hour	Summary of Events and Information	Remarks and references to Appendices
	Augt 21st		Usual Company Training.	
	22nd		Battalion Parade.	
	23rd		Interior Economy. 10 other ranks left for demobilization	
	24th		Usual Church Service. 3 other ranks left for civilian liquidation	
	25th		Lecture for 2 Companies. 1 Company firing 9mE on Pattisdorf range	
	26th		Usual Company training.	
	27th		One Company firing 9mE on Pattisdorf range. Remainder usual Coy training	
	28th		Usual Company Training.	
	29th		Companies at disposal of Coy. Commanders.	
	30th		Interior Economy	
Pattisdorf	31/8/19		Usual Church Service.	

Comdg. 12TH BN. LOYAL N. LANCS. REGT. (PIONEERS)

Lt. Col.
1st Aug. 1919 – 31st Aug. 1919.

Casualties
Officers to Hospital. Sick. 3
Oth. rank   "   "   71
Offrs from Hospital   3
oth ranks from "   60

STRENGTH
51 Officers
1247 other ranks

> 12 Bn LOYAL NORTH LANCS. REGT
> PIONEERS
> 2 9 SEP. 1919
> No /   A/949/9

To:- Lancashire Division "A"

        Herewith original copy of War Diary of month ending Sept. 30 please.

29/9/19.

        Bruce D____   Lieut. Colonel.
                             Commanding.
     12th Bn Loyal North Lancashire Regt.(Pioneers)

CONFIDENTIAL.

WAR DIARY.

OF

12TH. BN THE LOYAL NORTH LANCASHIRE REGIMENT.

1ST SEPTEMBER TO 30TH SEPTEMBER. 1919.

VOLUME. 40.

Army Form C. 2118.

WAR DIARY
or
INTELLIGENCE SUMMARY.
(Erase heading not required.)

12th Bn Loyal North Lancashire Regt. (Pioneers).

Place	Date	Hour	Summary of Events and Information	Remarks and references to Appendices
Infantry Barracks, Argelander Strasse, B O N N.	Sept. 1st.		DISTRIBUTION. The whole of the Battalion is quartered in the Barracks, Bonn. Usual Company Training. One Company firing G.M.C. on Dottendorf Range. Sec: Lieut C.H.Donnellan reported back from Army Commercial College, Cologne.	
	2nd.		Usual Company Training and Education.	
	3rd.		One Company firing on Dottendorf Range, remainder usual Company Training. 40 O.Rs to U.K. for demobilization.	
	4th.		Usual Company training, 40 O.Rs to U.K. for demobilization.	
	5th.		Battalion Parade.	
	6th.		Interior Economy and Commanding Officer's Inspection of Barracks, 6 O.Rs to U.K. for demobilization.	
	7th.		C. of E. Battalion Church Parade in Reuterstrasse Church. Usual R.C. and N.C.F. Services. Lieut Parkin and 5 O.Rs left for DROVE to take part in the Army Rifle Meeting.	
	8th.		One Company firing G.M.C. on Dottendorf Range, remainder usual Company Training. 20 O.Rs to U.K. for demobilization.	
	9th.		Usual Company Training and Education. 50 O.Rs to U.K. for demobilization.	
	10th.		One Company firing G.M.C. on Dottendorf Range, remainder usual Company Training. Lieut J. Dawson, 2/Lt S.Mullineux and 2/Lt J.H.Heap to U.K. for demobilization. 61 O.Rs to U.K. for demobilization.	
	11th.		Usual Company Training and Education. Lieut G.W.Slack, Lieut G.H.Tasker, 2/Lieut R.W.Robinson to U.K. for demobilization.	
	12th.		Battalion Parade. 18 O.Rs to U.K. for demobilization.	
	13th.		Interior Economy. Commanding Officer's Inspection of Barracks.	

Army Form C. 2118.

WAR DIARY
or
INTELLIGENCE SUMMARY.

(Erase heading not required.)

12th Bn Loyal North Lancashire Regt. (Pioneers).

Instructions regarding War Diaries and Intelligence Summaries are contained in F. S. Regs., Part II. and the Staff Manual respectively. Title pages will be prepared in manuscript.

Place	Date	Hour	Summary of Events and Information	Remarks and references to Appendices
Infantry Barracks, Argelander Strasse, BONN.	14th.		C. of E's Battalion Church Parade. Usual R.C. and N.C.F. Services.	
	15th.		One Company firing G.M.C. on Dettendorf Range, remainder usual Company Training. Lt-Col Murphy, W.H. to U.K. for demobilization. Major J.B.Dunn (H.L.I.) assumed command of the Battalion. 20 O.Rs to U.K. for Demobilization.	
	16th.		Usual Company Training and Education.	
	17th.		One Company firing G.M.C. on Dettendorf Range, remainder Company Training. Lecture by Hon. Crawford Vaughan, "America and Britain". Capt. A. Manning, M.M., Lieut L.Q. Henriques, 2/Lieut F.L. Parkin and 100 O.Rs to U.K. for Demob.	
	18th.		Usual Company Training and Education. Lieut J.G. Anderson and Lieut R.P. Hargreaves to U.K. for demobilization.	
	19th.		Battalion Route March. 200 O.Rs to U.K. for demobilization.	
	20th.		Interior Economy and Commanding Officer's Inspection of Barracks.	
	21st.		C. of Es Services in Barracks Theatre, usual R.C. and N.C.F. Services. 2/Lieut L. Stirling to U.K. for demobilization.	
	22nd.		One Company firing G.M.C. on Dettendorf Range, remainder usual Company Training. 2/Lieut H. Stephenson, M.M., and 60 O.Rs to U.K. for demobilization.	
	23rd.		Usual Company Training and Education.	
	24th.		Usual Company Training and Education. Lieut E. Williamson left for No.1 Concentration Camp, B.A.R. for duty as T.C.O.	
	25th.		Usual Company Training and Education.	

Army Form C. 2118.

WAR DIARY
or
INTELLIGENCE SUMMARY.

12th Bn Loyal North Lancashire Regt. (Pioneers).

(Erase heading not required.)

Instructions regarding War Diaries and Intelligence Summaries are contained in F. S. Regs., Part II. and the Staff Manual respectively. Title pages will be prepared in manuscript.

Place	Date	Hour	Summary of Events and Information.	Remarks and references to Appendices
Infantry Barracks, Argelander Strasse, B O N N.	26th.		Usual Company Training and Education and Interior Economy.	
	27th.		Interior Economy and Commanding Officers Inspection of Barracks.	
	28th.		Usual Church Services.	
	29th.		Company Training.	
	30th.		Company Training.	

CASUALTIES. 1st Septr. 1919 to 30th Septr. 1919.

Officers admitted to Hospital - Sick. 1.

Other Ranks admitted to Hospital - Sick. 29.

Officers returned to duty from Hospital 1.

Other Ranks returned to duty from Hospital. 26.

STRENGTH. 36. Officers. 591. Other Ranks.

Lt-Col,
Commanding,
12th Bn Loyal North Lancashire Regt. (Pioneers).

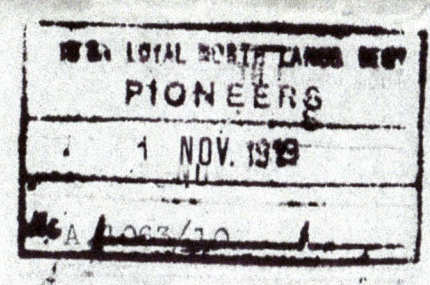

To:- Lancashire Division. "A"

        Herewith original Copy of War Diary of this Unit for Month-Ending 31st of October 1919.

                                        Lieut Colonel.
                                  Commanding,
          12th Bn Loyal North Lancashire Regiment. (Pioneers)

Army Form C. 2118.

WAR DIARY
or
INTELLIGENCE SUMMARY.
(Erase heading not required.)

12th Bn Loyal North Lancashire Regt.
(Pioneers)

Place	Date	Hour	Summary of Events and Information	Remarks and references to Appendices
Infantry Barracks, Argelander Strasse, BONN.	Oct. 1st.		Distribution. The whole of the Battalion is quartered in the Infantarie Caserne. Battalion re-organized on a two company basis to conserve man-power in view of the declining numbers of the Battalion. "C" Company dissolved and personnel merged into "A" and "B" Companies, the former under command of Capt C.A.Atkins and the latter under Capt. W.R.Harkess. "A" Company proceeded to Bonn to take over "Town Duties" from 13th King's Liverpool Regt and took up quarters in the University Buildings.	
	2nd.		Usual Company Training.	
	3rd.		Usual Company Training.	
	4th.		Interior Economy and Commanding Officer's Inspection of Barracks.	
	5th.		Usual Church Services. C. of E. Garrison Church, Bonn. R.C. Catholic Military Church, Bonn. Non. Conf Garrison Church, Bonn.	
	6th.		Usual Company Training and Education.	
	7th.		Usual Company Training and Education.	
	8th.		Usual Company Training and Education.	
	9th.		Usual Company Training and Education.	
	10th.		Usual Company Training.	
	11th.		Interior Economy and Commanding Officer's inspection of Barracks. 19 O.Rs to Conent for Demobilization.	
	12th.		Usual Church Services. C. of E. in Barrack Theatre. R. C. Catholic Military Church, Bonn. N. C. Garrison Church, Bonn. Capt. J.S.Flood and 25 O.Rs to Conent for Demob.	

Army Form C. 2118.

WAR DIARY
or
INTELLIGENCE-SUMMARY.

(Erase heading not required.)   12th Bn Loyal North Lancashire Regt. (Pioneers).

Instructions regarding War Diaries and Intelligence Summaries are contained in F. S. Regs., Part II. and the Staff Manual respectively. Title pages will be prepared in manuscript.

Place	Date	Hour	Summary of Events and Information	Remarks and references to Appendices
Infantry Barracks Argelander Strasse, BONN.	Octr. 13th.		Usual Company Training and Education. 2/Lieuts. R.P.Hargreavesand T.R.Smith and 20 O.Rs to Concent for Demob.	
	14th.		Usual Company Training and Education. Lieut J.P.Strong and 17 O.Rs to Concent for Demob.	
	15th.		Usual Company Training and Education.	
	16th.		Usual Company Training and Education.	
	17th.		"A" Company releived from Town Duties by 5th Border Regiment and are returned to Barracks. Battalion handed over Argelander Strasse, Barracks to 52nd King's Liverpool Regt., and moved into Museum Barracks vacated by 51st King's Liverpool Regt. 20 O.Rs to Concent for Demob.	
Museum Barracks Coblenzer Stradse, BONN.	18th.		Distribution. H.Q., A and B. Companies in Barracks. Transport Lines, Reuter Strasse. Cleaning up quarters and interior economy.	
	19th.		Usual Church Services. C.of E. Garrison Church, Bonn. R.C. Catholic Military Church, Bonn. N.C. Garrison Church, Bonn.	
	20th.		Usual Company Training and Education.	
	21st.		Usual Company Training and Education. 2/Lieut A.A.Peterkin to U.K. for 14 days leave. 4 O.Rs to Concent for demobilization.	
	22nd.		Usual Company Training and Education. Lieut C.H.Donnellan 14 days leave to France. 12 O.Rs to Concent for Demob.	
	23rd.		Usual Company Training and Education.	

Army Form C. 2118.

WAR DIARY
or
INTELLIGENCE SUMMARY.

(Erase heading not required.) 12th Bn Loyal North Lancashire Regt. (Pioneers).

Instructions regarding War Diaries and Intelligence Summaries are contained in F.S. Regs., Part II. and the Staff Manual respectively. Title pages will be prepared in manuscript.

Place	Date	Hour	Summary of Events and Information	Remarks and references to Appendices
Museum Barracks, Coblenzer Strasse, BONN.	Octr. 24th		Usual Company Training and Education. 12 O.Rs to Concert for Demob.	
	25th.		Interior Economy and Commanding Officer's Inspection of Barracks. Lieuts B.A.Macgowan, G.H.Rushton and 2/Lieut W.E.Knowles, M.M. to Concert for Demob. Took over Divisional Commander's Guard from 32nd M.G. Battalion.	
	26th.		Usual Church Services. C. of E. Recreation Room, Barracks. R. C. Catholic Military Church, Bonn. W. C. Garrison Church, Bonn. Took over Corps Commander's Guard Goods Station Guard and Endenicher Allee Guard. 2/Lieut H.V.Poole and 30 O.Rs to Concert for demob.	
	27th.		Practice "Action of troops in case of Riots in Bonn."	
	28th.		Training and P. and R.T. for employed men. Lieut. E.Williamson and 5 O.Rs to Concert for Demob.	
	29th.		Training and P. and R.T. for employed men.	
	30th.		Training and P. and R.T. for employed men.	
	31st.		Training and P. and R.T. for employed men. 3 O.Rs to Concert for Demob.	
			Casualties. 1st October to 30th October 1919.	
			Officers admitted to Hospital.- Nil Sick. O.Rs admitted to Hospital. 10.	
			Officers returned from Hospital. Nil. O.Rs returned from Hospital. 11. Strength. Officers. 25. Other Ranks. 388.	

Lieut-Colonel
Comdg 12th Bn Loyal North Lancashire Regt. (Pioneers).

www.ingramcontent.com/pod-product-compliance
Lightning Source LLC
Chambersburg PA
CBHW081454160426
43193CB00013B/2473